Navigating the Future of Pharmaceutical Marketing

Rizwan Raheem Ahmed, Ph.D.

DEDICATION

This book is dedicated to my Late Mother and Father who have provided me the financial, emotional, and Parental/Maternal opportunities to raise me, provided higher education and supported me in my initial professional life journey.

TABLE OF CONTENTS

ACKNOWLEDGMENTS

I Acknowledge my wife who has supported me during writing this book. She has also helped me to generate book cover and other relevant material on Photoshop. She has encouraged me all the way in my journey.

CHAPTER 1: INTRODUCTION

In the vast landscape of the pharmaceutical industry, where science and innovation intersect with healthcare needs, the role of marketing has never been more pivotal. This chapter marks the beginning of our journey into the intricate world of pharmaceutical marketing—a domain where the strategic crafting of campaigns can profoundly impact the well-being of individuals and the success of organizations.

Setting the Stage

The pharmaceutical industry stands at the crossroads of scientific breakthroughs and societal health demands. As we embark on this exploration of the Pharma Marketing Blueprint, it's essential to understand the unique challenges and opportunities that characterize this ever-evolving sector.

In recent years, the dynamics of pharmaceutical marketing

have undergone a transformative shift. Advances in technology, changing consumer behaviors, and stringent regulatory landscapes have redefined the playbook for creating compelling campaigns. Marketing in this industry is not merely about selling a product; it's about fostering a relationship between healthcare providers, patients, and the brands that strive to make a meaningful impact on health outcomes.

Objectives of the Book

The primary goal of this book is to serve as a comprehensive guide for professionals navigating the complex terrain of pharmaceutical marketing. Whether you're a seasoned marketer in the industry or someone seeking insights into this specialized field, each chapter is crafted to equip you with knowledge, strategies, and practical approaches.

Throughout the following pages, we will delve into the nuances of brand building, digital marketing strategies, multichannel approaches, patient-centric campaigns, and the critical role of data analytics. We'll navigate the labyrinth of regulatory compliance, explore emerging trends, and dissect case studies to distill lessons from successful campaigns.

Who Should Read This Book

"Navigating the Future of Pharmaceutical Marketing" is designed for a diverse audience, including pharmaceutical marketers, brand managers, healthcare professionals, and students aspiring to enter the field. The content is structured to cater to both seasoned industry veterans and those new to the world of pharmaceutical marketing.

Whether you're seeking a refresher on the fundamentals or aiming to stay ahead of the curve with the latest trends, each chapter offers actionable insights and a strategic framework that can be applied in various professional settings.

Navigating the Blueprint

As we progress through each chapter, envision this book as a roadmap—a blueprint, if you will. Each section is a crucial element contributing to the overall success of your pharmaceutical marketing endeavors. From understanding the industry landscape to harnessing the power of digital channels, we will systematically uncover the building blocks that create compelling campaigns.

This is not a one-size-fits-all guide but a dynamic blueprint that can be adapted to diverse pharmaceutical marketing contexts. Each reader is encouraged to engage with the material, question assumptions, and apply the principles in ways that align with their specific organizational goals and challenges.

So, let the journey begin. The Pharma Marketing Blueprint awaits, ready to illuminate the path to crafting campaigns that resonate, inspire, and ultimately contribute to the well-being of individuals around the globe.

CHAPTER 2: UNDERSTANDING THE PHARMA LANDSCAPE

In the vast and dynamic landscape of pharmaceuticals, understanding the nuances of the industry is fundamental to effective marketing. This chapter serves as a compass, guiding readers through the intricacies, challenges, and opportunities that define the pharmaceutical landscape.

Current Trends and Challenges

Shifting Paradigms

The pharmaceutical industry is witnessing paradigm shifts, driven by advancements in medical science, changes in consumer behavior, and evolving healthcare ecosystems. We explore these shifts and their implications for marketers, acknowledging the dual role of innovation and adaptation.

Regulatory Hurdles

Navigating the regulatory landscape is a constant challenge in pharmaceutical marketing. From stringent approval processes to compliance with advertising regulations, marketers must be well-versed in the legal framework that governs their campaigns.

Market Analysis and Segmentation

Data-Driven Insights

Market analysis is not just about understanding the present; it's about predicting the future. We delve into the importance of data-driven decision-making, utilizing market research, and leveraging analytics to gain actionable insights.

Patient-Centric Segmentation

In an era of personalized medicine, segmentation goes beyond demographics. We explore the concept of patient-centric segmentation, acknowledging the diversity of patient needs and tailoring marketing strategies accordingly.

Global Healthcare Landscape

Globalization of Healthcare

The pharmaceutical market is increasingly global, with

opportunities and challenges spanning across borders. We examine the implications of globalization, from market expansion to cultural considerations in marketing campaigns.

Access to Medicines

Ensuring access to medicines is a crucial aspect of pharmaceutical marketing. We discuss initiatives, challenges, and the ethical imperative of balancing profit motives with the imperative to address global health needs.

Case Studies: Learning from the Landscape

Success Stories

Real-world case studies offer insights into successful campaigns that navigated industry challenges. By examining these cases, readers can glean practical strategies and approaches applicable to their own marketing endeavors.

Looking Ahead

As we conclude this chapter, we cast a gaze into the future of the pharmaceutical landscape. What trends will shape the industry? How will societal shifts impact healthcare consumption? By understanding the present and anticipating the future, marketers can position themselves to craft campaigns that resonate in an ever-evolving landscape.

Join us as we unravel the layers of the pharmaceutical landscape, seeking to equip marketers with the knowledge and foresight needed to navigate the complexities and seize the opportunities that lie ahead.

CHAPTER 3: BUILDING A STRONG FOUNDATION

In the intricate world of pharmaceutical marketing, building a strong foundation is akin to laying the groundwork for a structure that can withstand the tests of time and market dynamics. This chapter focuses on the essential elements of brand building, target audience definition, and the crafting of a compelling value proposition.

Establishing Brand Identity and Positioning

The Power of Branding

A pharmaceutical brand is not merely a logo or a product; it embodies a promise, a commitment to health and well-being. We explore the strategic nuances of brand identity, discussing the elements that contribute to a memorable and impactful pharmaceutical brand.

Positioning for Success

In a crowded market, effective positioning is paramount. We delve into the art and science of positioning pharmaceutical brands to resonate with healthcare professionals, patients, and other stakeholders. Case studies illuminate successful positioning strategies employed by industry leaders.

Defining Target Audiences and Patient Personas

Precision Targeting

Gone are the days of one-size-fits-all marketing. We examine the importance of defining specific target audiences within the healthcare professional and patient realms. The concept of patient personas is introduced, emphasizing the need for a nuanced understanding of patient needs, preferences, and behaviors.

Healthcare Professional Engagement

Building strong relationships with healthcare professionals is a cornerstone of pharmaceutical marketing. We explore strategies for effective engagement, understanding the challenges faced by healthcare providers, and tailoring campaigns to address their needs.

Crafting a Compelling Value Proposition

Beyond the Pill

The pharmaceutical value proposition extends beyond the efficacy of a drug. We discuss the concept of "beyond the pill" marketing, where brands offer additional value through services, support programs, and educational initiatives. This approach fosters loyalty and differentiation in a competitive landscape.

Communicating Value Effectively

Crafting a compelling value proposition is one step; effectively communicating it is another. We explore communication strategies, emphasizing the importance of clear, transparent, and empathetic messaging that resonates with both healthcare professionals and patients.

Case Studies: Foundation in Action

Notable Examples

Case studies bring theory to life, showcasing how successful pharmaceutical brands have built strong foundations. By analyzing these cases, readers gain insights into the practical application of brand identity, positioning, audience definition, and value proposition development.

Future-Proofing the Foundation

As we conclude this chapter, we consider how the foundational elements discussed can adapt to future trends and challenges. Building a strong foundation is not a one-time endeavor; it's an ongoing process of evolution and adaptation in response to an ever-changing pharmaceutical landscape.

Join us as we lay the bricks of a robust foundation, setting the stage for strategic pharmaceutical marketing that stands resilient amidst the complexities of the industry.

CHAPTER 4: NAVIGATING THE DIGITAL FRONTIER

In an era where digital technologies permeate every aspect of our lives, pharmaceutical marketing must adeptly navigate the digital frontier to reach and engage with healthcare professionals and patients. This chapter explores the transformative impact of digital marketing strategies, from online presence to data-driven decision-making.

The Evolution of Digital Marketing in Pharmaceuticals

From Traditional to Digital

The journey from traditional marketing channels to the digital landscape is charted, highlighting the pivotal moments and technologies that reshaped pharmaceutical marketing. We explore the opportunities and challenges that accompany this paradigm shift.

The Rise of E-Health

E-health initiatives, including online health information platforms, patient portals, and telemedicine, are transforming the healthcare landscape. We discuss how pharmaceutical marketers can align their strategies with these emerging trends to enhance brand visibility and patient engagement.

Establishing a Robust Online Presence

Website Optimization

A pharmaceutical brand's website is often the first point of contact for healthcare professionals and patients. We delve into the principles of website optimization, ensuring that online platforms effectively communicate the brand's identity, value proposition, and key messages.

Search Engine Optimization (SEO)

Visibility in online searches is critical for pharmaceutical brands. We explore the fundamentals of SEO, from keyword optimization to content strategies, empowering marketers to enhance their online discoverability and reach a wider audience.

Leveraging Social Media for Engagement

Social Media Landscape

Social media platforms provide avenues for real-time engagement and information dissemination. We analyze the social media landscape in pharmaceutical marketing, examining successful campaigns and the ethical considerations inherent in these interactive spaces.

Influencer Marketing in Healthcare

The emergence of healthcare influencers presents new opportunities for brands to connect with audiences authentically. We explore the dynamics of influencer marketing in healthcare, discussing best practices and potential pitfalls.

Data-Driven Decision-Making

Harnessing Big Data

The pharmaceutical industry generates vast amounts of data. We discuss how marketers can harness big data to gain actionable insights, personalize campaigns, and measure the impact of their digital strategies.

Analytics and Metrics

Effective digital marketing relies on analytics and metrics

for continuous improvement. We explore key performance indicators (KPIs), tools for measurement, and strategies for optimizing digital campaigns based on data-driven insights.

Case Studies: Digital Success Stories

Exemplary Campaigns

Real-world case studies showcase pharmaceutical brands that have successfully navigated the digital frontier. By dissecting these campaigns, readers gain practical insights into the application of digital strategies for enhanced brand visibility and engagement.

Looking Ahead: The Future of Digital Marketing

As we conclude this chapter, we cast our gaze toward the future of digital marketing in pharmaceuticals. Emerging technologies, evolving consumer behaviors, and regulatory considerations shape the trajectory of digital strategies. By anticipating these changes, marketers can position themselves for continued success in the digital era.

Join us as we explore the digital frontier, unraveling the strategies that propel pharmaceutical marketing into a new realm of possibilities and engagement.

CHAPTER 5: BUILDING STRATEGIC PARTNERSHIPS

In the dynamic landscape of pharmaceutical marketing, strategic partnerships are key to unlocking synergies, fostering innovation, and expanding the reach of healthcare solutions. This chapter delves into the art and science of building meaningful partnerships, from collaborations with healthcare professionals to alliances with industry stakeholders.

Collaborating with Healthcare Professionals

Establishing Trust-Based Relationships

Trust is the bedrock of collaborations with healthcare professionals. We explore strategies for building and maintaining trust, understanding the needs of healthcare professionals, and aligning brand objectives with their expertise.

Educational Initiatives

Collaborative educational initiatives benefit both pharmaceutical brands and healthcare professionals. We discuss the design and implementation of educational programs that contribute to professional development while enhancing brand credibility.

Patient Advocacy and Support

Empowering Patient Advocates

Patient advocacy plays a crucial role in pharmaceutical marketing. We examine the importance of identifying and collaborating with patient advocates, organizations, and support groups to amplify the patient voice and enhance brand authenticity.

Support Programs and Resources

Developing support programs and resources for patients goes beyond medication. We explore how pharmaceutical brands can provide valuable resources, tools, and support networks to empower patients on their healthcare journeys.

Industry Collaborations and Alliances

Cross-Industry Collaborations

Innovation often thrives at the intersection of industries. We discuss the potential for pharmaceutical brands to collaborate with technology, biotech, and other sectors to bring novel solutions to market.

Public-Private Partnerships

Public-private partnerships are instrumental in addressing global health challenges. We explore how pharmaceutical companies can engage with governments, NGOs, and international organizations to contribute to healthcare initiatives while advancing their strategic goals.

Stakeholder Engagement and Management

Identifying Key Stakeholders

A strategic approach to stakeholder engagement involves identifying and understanding key players in the pharmaceutical ecosystem. We discuss methods for stakeholder mapping, recognizing their influence, and tailoring engagement strategies accordingly.

Ethical Considerations in Partnerships

Ethical considerations are paramount in building partnerships. We explore the ethical principles that guide collaborations, emphasizing transparency, integrity, and a commitment to the well-being of all stakeholders involved.

Case Studies: Partnership Success Stories

Transformative Collaborations

Examining real-world examples, we showcase partnerships that have yielded transformative outcomes. From healthcare professional collaborations to cross-industry alliances, these case studies offer insights into the dynamics of successful partnerships.

Future-Proofing Collaborations

As we conclude this chapter, we look ahead to the future of strategic partnerships in pharmaceutical marketing. Anticipating trends, adapting to regulatory changes, and fostering a culture of collaboration are essential for building resilient and future-proof partnerships.

Join us on a journey through the realm of strategic partnerships, where collaboration becomes a strategic imperative for pharmaceutical brands seeking to innovate, expand their impact, and contribute meaningfully to the evolving healthcare landscape.

CHAPTER 6: ADAPTING TO REGULATORY LANDSCAPES

In the pharmaceutical industry, navigating complex regulatory landscapes is intrinsic to ensuring compliance, maintaining ethical standards, and bringing innovative healthcare solutions to market. This chapter explores the nuances of regulatory affairs and the strategies pharmaceutical marketers employ to adapt to evolving regulatory frameworks.

Understanding Regulatory Dynamics

The Regulatory Ecosystem

The pharmaceutical regulatory landscape is multifaceted, encompassing local, regional, and international regulations. We delve into the dynamics of regulatory bodies, their roles, and the factors influencing the evolution of pharmaceutical regulations.

Impact on Marketing Strategies

Regulatory requirements shape the boundaries within which pharmaceutical marketing operates. We discuss how marketers can align their strategies with regulatory expectations, ensuring promotional activities adhere to ethical standards and legal compliance.

Navigating Global and Local Regulations

Harmonization Efforts

Harmonization initiatives seek to align regulations across borders, facilitating global drug development and marketing. We explore the impact of international harmonization on pharmaceutical marketing strategies and the challenges of navigating diverse regulatory environments.

Tailoring Strategies to Local Contexts

While global standards provide a framework, local regulations present unique challenges. We discuss the importance of tailoring marketing strategies to local contexts, considering cultural nuances, healthcare systems, and regional regulatory variations.

Compliance and Ethics in Marketing

Promoting Ethical Marketing Practices

Maintaining ethical standards is a cornerstone of pharmaceutical marketing. We explore the ethical considerations in promotional activities, emphasizing transparency, accuracy, and the ethical promotion of healthcare products.

Regulatory Compliance in Digital Marketing

The digital landscape introduces new challenges in regulatory compliance. We discuss how pharmaceutical marketers can navigate the intricacies of digital marketing, including online advertising, social media, and data privacy, while remaining compliant with regulations.

Regulatory Submissions and Approvals

Marketing Authorization Applications

Securing marketing authorization is a pivotal milestone. We guide marketers through the process of preparing and submitting marketing authorization applications, understanding the documentation required, and collaborating with regulatory agencies.

Post-Approval Commitments

Post-approval commitments are integral to regulatory compliance. We explore the types of commitments, ranging from pharmacovigilance to real-world evidence generation, and how marketers can fulfill these obligations while maintaining a strong market presence.

Case Studies: Regulatory Challenges and Solutions

Navigating Complexities

Real-world case studies illuminate the challenges pharmaceutical marketers have faced in the regulatory arena. By examining these cases, readers gain insights into the strategies employed to overcome regulatory hurdles and maintain successful marketing campaigns.

Anticipating Regulatory Trends

As we conclude this chapter, we look to the future of pharmaceutical regulations. Anticipating regulatory trends, staying informed about evolving requirements, and proactively adapting marketing strategies are essential for success in an ever-changing regulatory landscape.

Join us as we unravel the intricacies of regulatory affairs, providing pharmaceutical marketers with the knowledge and strategies needed to navigate complex regulatory landscapes while ensuring compliance, ethical standards, and successful market access.

CHAPTER 7: EMBRACING INNOVATION IN HEALTHCARE MARKETING

In the fast-paced world of healthcare marketing, embracing innovation is not just a strategic choice; it is a necessity for staying ahead in a competitive landscape. This chapter explores the dynamic intersection of healthcare and technology, showcasing how innovation can revolutionize marketing strategies and redefine the patient experience.

The Convergence of Healthcare and Technology

Digital Health Revolution

The digital health revolution is reshaping the healthcare industry. We explore the transformative impact of digital technologies, including telemedicine, wearables, and health apps, and how pharmaceutical marketers can integrate these innovations into their strategies.

AI and Machine Learning in Healthcare

Artificial Intelligence (AI) and machine learning are driving advancements in diagnostics, drug discovery, and patient care. This section examines the role of AI in healthcare marketing, from personalized messaging to data-driven insights.

Personalization and Patient-Centric Approaches

Tailoring Marketing to Individual Patients

Personalization is no longer a buzzword; it's a strategic imperative. We delve into the power of personalized marketing, exploring how pharmaceutical brands can tailor their messages to resonate with individual patients, fostering engagement and brand loyalty.

Patient Journey Mapping

Understanding the patient journey is essential for crafting effective marketing strategies. We guide marketers through the process of patient journey mapping, identifying touchpoints for engagement and optimizing the overall patient experience.

Virtual and Augmented Reality in Healthcare

Immersive Healthcare Experiences

Virtual and augmented reality offer immersive experiences that can educate, engage, and empower patients. We explore the applications of these technologies in healthcare marketing, from virtual product demonstrations to augmented reality patient education.

Enhancing Medical Education

Innovations in virtual and augmented reality extend beyond patient engagement. We discuss how pharmaceutical marketers can leverage these technologies to enhance medical education for healthcare professionals, creating impactful learning experiences.

Blockchain in Healthcare Marketing

Ensuring Transparency and Trust

Blockchain technology has the potential to revolutionize data security and transparency in healthcare. We examine how pharmaceutical marketers can use blockchain to build trust, secure data, and enhance the integrity of marketing initiatives.

Supply Chain and Product Traceability

Beyond marketing, blockchain plays a crucial role in ensuring the authenticity and traceability of pharmaceutical products. We explore how blockchain technology can be integrated into supply chain processes and communicated to build consumer trust.

Interactive and Gamified Campaigns

Gamification for Patient Engagement

Gamification has proven to be a powerful tool for engaging patients in their healthcare journeys. We discuss how pharmaceutical marketers can implement gamified campaigns to educate, motivate, and reward patients for positive health behaviors.

Interactive Content Strategies

Interactive content, from quizzes to virtual events, enhances user engagement. We explore how interactive content strategies can be applied in pharmaceutical marketing, fostering a two-way communication flow with healthcare professionals and patients.

Case Studies: Innovations that Resonate

Trailblazing Campaigns

Real-world case studies showcase pharmaceutical brands that have successfully embraced innovation in their marketing endeavors. By dissecting these campaigns, readers gain practical insights into the application of innovative strategies for impactful results.

The Road Ahead: Embracing Continuous Innovation

As we conclude this chapter, we reflect on the ever-evolving landscape of healthcare marketing. Embracing a culture of continuous innovation, staying abreast of emerging technologies, and being agile in adapting strategies are key to thriving in the dynamic intersection of healthcare and innovation.

Embark on a journey through the cutting-edge realm of healthcare marketing innovation, where forward-thinking strategies and emerging technologies converge to shape the future of patient engagement, brand differentiation, and overall industry impact.

CHAPTER 8: MEASURING IMPACT AND ROI IN PHARMACEUTICAL MARKETING

In the realm of pharmaceutical marketing, effective measurement and the ability to demonstrate Return on Investment (ROI) are critical for optimizing strategies, justifying budgets, and ensuring sustainable success. This chapter delves into the methodologies, key performance indicators (KPIs), and tools used to measure the impact of pharmaceutical marketing efforts.

Establishing Clear Objectives and Key Performance Indicators

Defining Measurable Objectives

Clear and measurable objectives are the foundation of effective measurement. We guide pharmaceutical marketers in establishing objectives that align with overall business goals and are quantifiable for assessment.

Identifying Key Performance Indicators (KPIs)

Choosing the right KPIs is essential for accurate measurement. We explore the diverse range of KPIs applicable to pharmaceutical marketing, from brand awareness metrics to lead generation and conversion rates.

Utilizing Analytical Tools and Technologies

Data Analytics Platforms

Data analytics platforms empower marketers to derive actionable insights from vast datasets. We discuss the functionalities of leading analytics tools and how pharmaceutical marketers can leverage these technologies to measure and optimize campaigns.

Customer Relationship Management (CRM) Systems

CRM systems play a pivotal role in tracking and managing

customer interactions. We explore how pharmaceutical companies can integrate CRM systems into their marketing strategies to enhance customer engagement and measure the impact on customer relationships.

Attribution Modeling for Multi-Channel Campaigns

Understanding Attribution Models

Multi-channel marketing requires sophisticated attribution models to assign value to each touchpoint in the customer journey. We discuss various attribution models, including first-touch, last-touch, and multi-touch, and their application in pharmaceutical marketing.

Challenges and Solutions in Attribution

Attribution modeling comes with challenges, especially in the healthcare sector. We address common challenges and provide solutions for accurate attribution, considering factors such as patient privacy, long sales cycles, and multi-stakeholder decision-making.

Real-Time Monitoring and Adaptive Strategies

Real-Time Analytics

Real-time monitoring allows marketers to adapt strategies on the fly. We explore the importance of real-time analytics in pharmaceutical marketing, providing examples of how companies can use instantaneous insights to optimize ongoing campaigns.

A/B Testing and Continuous Improvement

A/B testing is a powerful method for refining marketing strategies. We guide pharmaceutical marketers through the principles of A/B testing, emphasizing continuous improvement based on data-driven insights.

Compliance in Data Measurement and Reporting

Ensuring Data Security and Privacy

Pharmaceutical marketing involves handling sensitive health data, necessitating a strong focus on compliance. We discuss the measures companies should take to ensure data security, privacy, and compliance with regulations such as HIPAA.

Transparent Reporting Practices

Transparent reporting builds trust with stakeholders. We explore best practices in reporting, including clear communication of methodologies, data sources, and limitations, ensuring transparency in measurement and reporting practices.

Case Studies: Demonstrating Successful Measurement Strategies

Measuring Success in Diverse Campaigns

Real-world case studies highlight pharmaceutical marketing campaigns that have successfully measured and demonstrated ROI. By examining these cases, readers gain insights into effective measurement strategies across different marketing contexts.

Strategic Adaptation Based on Measurement Insights

As we conclude this chapter, we emphasize the iterative nature of measurement and the importance of strategic adaptation based on insights. Pharmaceutical marketers are encouraged to use measurement data not just for reporting but as a strategic compass for future campaigns and optimizations.

Embark on a journey of measurement mastery in pharmaceutical marketing, where clear objectives, sophisticated tools, and strategic adaptation converge to demonstrate impact, optimize campaigns, and pave the way for continuous improvement in the dynamic landscape of healthcare promotion.

CHAPTER 9: NAVIGATING REGULATORY CHALLENGES IN PHARMACEUTICAL MARKETING

The pharmaceutical industry operates within a complex regulatory landscape, where stringent guidelines aim to ensure the safety, accuracy, and ethicality of marketing practices. This chapter delves into the intricacies of regulatory challenges in pharmaceutical marketing, offering guidance on compliance, ethical considerations, and strategies for navigating the evolving regulatory environment.

The Regulatory Landscape: An Overview

Key Regulatory Bodies and Guidelines

Understanding the regulatory bodies and guidelines governing pharmaceutical marketing is essential. We provide an overview of key organizations such as the Food and Drug Administration (FDA), European Medicines Agency (EMA), and other global regulatory bodies shaping marketing standards.

Evolving Regulatory Trends

The regulatory landscape is dynamic, with continuous updates and changes. We explore current and emerging trends in pharmaceutical marketing regulations, including increased scrutiny of digital channels, data privacy concerns, and the impact of global events on regulatory priorities.

Marketing Authorization and Product Claims

Navigating the Approval Process

The journey from product development to market authorization involves regulatory scrutiny. We guide pharmaceutical marketers through the intricacies of the approval process, emphasizing the importance of aligning marketing materials with approved product claims.

Communicating Product Efficacy and Safety

Ensuring accurate and balanced communication of product efficacy and safety is a paramount consideration. We delve into best practices for crafting promotional materials that meet regulatory standards while effectively conveying the benefits and risks of pharmaceutical products.

Direct-to-Consumer Advertising (DTCA)

Regulations and Ethical Considerations

Direct-to-consumer advertising presents unique challenges and opportunities. We explore the regulations and ethical considerations associated with DTCA, addressing issues such as fair balance, transparency, and the role of healthcare professionals in consumer-directed campaigns.

Navigating Digital Channels in DTCA

In an era dominated by digital communication, pharmaceutical marketers must navigate the specific challenges of online channels in DTCA. We discuss strategies for compliant and ethical engagement through websites, social media, and other digital platforms.

Data Privacy and Compliance

Patient Privacy and Consent

The use of patient data in pharmaceutical marketing

demands rigorous adherence to privacy regulations. We delve into the principles of patient privacy, informed consent, and the evolving landscape of data protection laws globally.

Managing Data Across Borders

In a globalized industry, managing data across borders requires a nuanced understanding of international data protection laws. We provide insights into the complexities of cross-border data transfer and strategies for compliance in a diverse regulatory environment.

Ethical Marketing Practices

Upholding Ethical Standards

Ethical marketing is foundational to maintaining public trust and industry credibility. We explore ethical considerations in pharmaceutical marketing, addressing issues such as transparency, integrity, and responsible engagement with healthcare professionals and consumers.

Industry Self-Regulation Initiatives

Beyond external regulations, industry self-regulation initiatives play a role in upholding ethical standards. We examine initiatives led by pharmaceutical associations and organizations aimed at promoting responsible marketing practices within the industry.

Crisis Management and Regulatory Response

Proactive Crisis Planning

Preparedness for potential crises is a crucial aspect of regulatory compliance. We guide pharmaceutical companies in developing proactive crisis management plans, including rapid response strategies and communication protocols.

Collaborating with Regulatory Authorities

In times of crisis, collaboration with regulatory authorities is paramount. We discuss strategies for open communication, transparency, and cooperation with regulatory bodies to navigate challenges and rebuild trust.

Case Studies: Learning from Regulatory Experiences

Navigating Regulatory Challenges Successfully

Real-world case studies provide insights into how pharmaceutical companies have navigated regulatory challenges effectively. By examining these cases, readers gain practical lessons and strategies for mitigating risks and ensuring compliance.

The Road Ahead: Adapting to Regulatory Evolution

As we conclude this chapter, we emphasize the importance of continuous adaptation to regulatory changes. Pharmaceutical marketers are encouraged to stay informed, engage in ongoing education, and foster a culture of compliance to navigate the evolving regulatory landscape successfully.

Embark on a comprehensive exploration of regulatory challenges in pharmaceutical marketing, where compliance, ethics, and strategic navigation converge to ensure the integrity and success of marketing initiatives in an industry governed by strict regulations and evolving standards.

CHAPTER 10: THE FUTURE LANDSCAPE OF PHARMACEUTICAL MARKETING

The pharmaceutical marketing landscape is undergoing unprecedented transformations driven by technological advancements, shifting consumer behaviors, and evolving healthcare paradigms. In this final chapter, we explore the emerging trends, innovative strategies, and future considerations that will shape the trajectory of pharmaceutical marketing in the years to come.

Digital Transformation in Pharmaceutical Marketing

The Rise of Digital Health Platforms

Digital health platforms are reshaping patient engagement and healthcare delivery. We examine the integration of pharmaceutical marketing into digital health ecosystems, exploring opportunities for personalized communication, patient education, and real-time interaction.

Artificial Intelligence and Data Analytics

Artificial Intelligence (AI) and advanced data analytics are becoming integral to pharmaceutical marketing strategies. We discuss how AI can enhance personalized marketing, improve targeting precision, and optimize campaign outcomes while navigating ethical considerations and privacy concerns.

Patient-Centric Approaches

Empowering Patients through Information

The empowered patient is at the center of the future healthcare landscape. We explore strategies for pharmaceutical marketers to empower patients through informative content, educational initiatives, and tools that enhance health literacy and shared decision-making.

Patient Communities and Social Engagement

Building patient communities and fostering social engagement are pivotal for pharmaceutical brands. We delve into the creation of online communities, social media strategies, and patient advocacy programs that facilitate meaningful connections and dialogue.

Personalized Medicine and Targeted Marketing

The Era of Personalized Medicine

Advancements in genomics and personalized medicine are reshaping healthcare. We discuss how pharmaceutical marketers can align with this paradigm shift, engaging in targeted marketing approaches that resonate with specific patient populations based on genetic and molecular profiles.

Influencer Marketing in Healthcare

Influencer marketing extends into the healthcare domain. We explore the ethical considerations and opportunities for collaboration with healthcare professionals, patient advocates, and influencers to amplify pharmaceutical marketing messages and build trust.

Regulatory and Ethical Considerations in the Future

Anticipating Regulatory Changes

The dynamic nature of the pharmaceutical industry requires marketers to anticipate and adapt to regulatory changes. We provide insights into proactive strategies for staying ahead of evolving regulations and maintaining compliance in a rapidly changing landscape.

Ethical Marketing in the Digital Age

As digital channels play an increasing role in pharmaceutical marketing, maintaining ethical standards becomes paramount. We discuss the ethical considerations specific to digital platforms and strategies for ethical marketing in the era of rapid technological innovation.

Globalization and Market Access

Expanding Market Reach

Globalization offers opportunities for expanding market reach. We explore considerations for pharmaceutical marketers entering new markets, including cultural nuances, regulatory variations, and strategies for establishing a global brand presence.

Access to Medicines and Patient Affordability

Ensuring access to medicines while addressing patient affordability is a critical consideration. We examine strategies for pharmaceutical companies to balance commercial interests with social responsibility, fostering access to life-changing medications.

Sustainability and Corporate Social Responsibility

The Role of Pharma in Sustainable Healthcare

The pharmaceutical industry plays a pivotal role in sustainable healthcare. We discuss the integration of sustainability and corporate social responsibility (CSR) into pharmaceutical marketing strategies, aligning business goals with societal and environmental impact.

Continuous Learning and Adaptation

Embracing a Culture of Continuous Learning

In a rapidly evolving landscape, a culture of continuous learning is essential. We provide guidance on fostering a mindset of adaptability, investing in professional development, and staying abreast of emerging trends to remain competitive in pharmaceutical marketing.

Reflections and Looking Ahead

As we conclude this book, we reflect on the transformative journey through the diverse facets of pharmaceutical marketing. The future holds unprecedented opportunities and challenges, and pharmaceutical marketers are encouraged to embrace innovation, uphold ethical standards, and contribute to shaping a future where healthcare communication is informative, patient-centric, and socially responsible.

Embark on a visionary exploration of the future landscape

of pharmaceutical marketing, where digital innovation, patient empowerment, global considerations, and ethical practices converge to define a dynamic and impactful future for the pharmaceutical industry.

CHAPTER 11: BEYOND MARKETING: HOLISTIC STRATEGIES FOR PHARMA SUCCESS

The evolving landscape of the pharmaceutical industry requires a holistic approach that extends beyond traditional marketing paradigms. In this chapter, we explore multifaceted strategies that encompass diverse facets of pharmaceutical operations, fostering success in an environment shaped by innovation, patient-centricity, and global considerations.

Integrated Product Lifecycle Management

From Development to Commercialization

Integrated product lifecycle management is crucial for pharmaceutical success. We delve into strategies for seamless coordination across the product lifecycle, from early development stages to commercialization, ensuring a cohesive and efficient approach that maximizes product potential.

Collaborative Cross-Functional Teams

Breaking down silos and fostering collaboration across cross-functional teams is essential. We discuss the importance of interdisciplinary collaboration, where professionals from research and development, marketing, regulatory affairs, and other departments work together harmoniously to achieve shared objectives.

Patient-Centric Product Design

Understanding Patient Needs

Incorporating patient perspectives into product design is paramount. We explore methodologies for understanding patient needs, preferences, and challenges, informing the development of pharmaceutical products that align with patient expectations and enhance overall healthcare experiences.

Human-Centered Design Principles

Human-centered design principles guide the creation of patient-centric solutions. We discuss how applying these principles to pharmaceutical product design can result in innovations that not only meet medical criteria but also resonate with users on a human level.

Global Market Access and Distribution

Navigating Regulatory Diversities

Expanding global market access requires navigating diverse regulatory landscapes. We provide insights into strategies for approaching regulatory variations in different regions, ensuring compliance, and optimizing market entry for pharmaceutical products.

Efficient Supply Chain Management

Efficient supply chain management is critical for timely

and cost-effective distribution. We explore best practices in supply chain optimization, including leveraging technology, ensuring product integrity, and maintaining flexibility to adapt to dynamic market demands.

Innovation in Research and Development

Embracing Technological Advancements

Innovation in research and development goes beyond traditional approaches. We discuss the integration of cutting-edge technologies such as artificial intelligence, machine learning, and data analytics in R&D processes, accelerating drug discovery and development.

Collaborative Research Partnerships

Collaborative research partnerships foster innovation. We explore strategies for establishing effective collaborations with academic institutions, research organizations, and other industry players to drive advancements in pharmaceutical research and development.

Corporate Social Responsibility (CSR) in Pharma

Beyond Compliance: A Commitment to Society

Corporate social responsibility is integral to pharmaceutical success. We delve into how pharmaceutical companies can go beyond mere compliance, actively engaging in initiatives that contribute to social welfare, healthcare accessibility, and community well-being.

Ethical Clinical Trial Practices

Ethical clinical trial practices are a cornerstone of CSR. We discuss the importance of conducting clinical trials with transparency, integrity, and a commitment to patient welfare, aligning research activities with ethical principles and societal expectations.

Continuous Learning and Development

Building a Learning Organization

The pharmaceutical industry's dynamic nature necessitates continuous learning. We explore strategies for cultivating a learning organization culture, where employees are empowered to stay abreast of industry developments, embrace innovation, and contribute to the organization's success.

Professional Development Initiatives

Investing in professional development initiatives is key to building a skilled workforce. We discuss the implementation of training programs, mentorship initiatives, and other professional development strategies that enhance employee capabilities and contribute to organizational excellence.

Adapting to Societal and Environmental Trends

Proactive Environmental Stewardship

Pharmaceutical companies can proactively contribute to environmental stewardship. We explore sustainability practices, waste reduction initiatives, and strategies for minimizing the environmental impact of pharmaceutical operations, aligning business goals with ecological responsibility.

Addressing Societal Health Challenges

Beyond product-specific initiatives, pharmaceutical companies can address broader societal health challenges. We discuss strategies for engaging in public health initiatives, supporting healthcare infrastructure development, and contributing to the resolution of critical health issues.

The Future of Pharma: A Holistic Vision

As we conclude this chapter, we reflect on the holistic vision necessary for the future of the pharmaceutical industry. By embracing integrated strategies that transcend traditional marketing boundaries, pharmaceutical companies can position themselves for sustained success in a dynamic and ever-evolving landscape.

Embark on a comprehensive exploration of holistic strategies for pharmaceutical success, where integrated approaches encompassing product lifecycle management, patient-centric design, global market access, innovation in research and development, corporate social responsibility, continuous learning, and adaptability converge to shape a resilient and impactful future for the pharmaceutical industry.

CHAPTER 12: NAVIGATING CHALLENGES AND SEIZING OPPORTUNITIES

In the final chapter of this comprehensive guide, we address the challenges and opportunities that pharmaceutical professionals may encounter in the dynamic landscape of the industry. By understanding and effectively navigating these factors, stakeholders can position themselves for success and contribute to the advancement of healthcare.

Regulatory Complexities in the Pharmaceutical Landscape

Evolving Regulatory Standards

The pharmaceutical industry operates within a framework of evolving regulatory standards. We explore the challenges posed by shifting regulations, emphasizing the importance of staying informed, adapting compliance strategies, and fostering proactive regulatory engagement.

Global Harmonization Initiatives

Global harmonization initiatives aim to streamline regulatory processes. We discuss the opportunities and challenges associated with global harmonization, including the potential for increased efficiency and market access, balanced with the need to address divergent regulatory requirements.

Healthcare Access and Affordability

Balancing Commercial Interests with Social Responsibility

Ensuring access to medicines while addressing affordability is a delicate balance. We explore strategies for pharmaceutical companies to align commercial interests with social responsibility, contributing to improved healthcare access without compromising financial viability.

Innovations in Access Programs

Innovative access programs play a pivotal role in expanding healthcare reach. We discuss successful models of access programs, such as tiered pricing, patient assistance programs, and collaborations with non-profit organizations, highlighting their impact on patient access.

Technological Disruptions in Healthcare

Embracing Digital Transformation

Technological disruptions, including digital health platforms and telemedicine, are reshaping healthcare delivery. We explore how pharmaceutical companies can embrace digital transformation, leveraging technology to enhance patient engagement, streamline clinical trials, and improve healthcare outcomes.

Cybersecurity Challenges

As the industry embraces digital solutions, cybersecurity becomes paramount. We delve into the cybersecurity challenges facing pharmaceutical companies, providing insights into safeguarding sensitive data, protecting intellectual property, and maintaining the integrity of digital systems.

Shifting Patient Expectations and Empowerment

The Informed and Empowered Patient

Patients are increasingly informed and empowered in their healthcare decisions. We discuss how pharmaceutical professionals can adapt to this shift, emphasizing transparent communication, patient education initiatives, and collaborative approaches that prioritize shared decision-making.

Patient Advocacy and Partnerships

Building partnerships with patient advocacy groups is essential. We explore the opportunities for pharmaceutical companies to collaborate with patient advocates, ensuring that the patient voice is integrated into drug development, access programs, and healthcare policy discussions.

Supply Chain Resilience and Global Logistics

Lessons from Supply Chain Disruptions

The COVID-19 pandemic highlighted vulnerabilities in global supply chains. We analyze lessons learned from supply chain disruptions, emphasizing the importance of building resilient supply chains, embracing digital technologies, and fostering collaboration across the supply network.

Sustainable and Ethical Sourcing Practices

Sustainable and ethical sourcing practices contribute to supply chain resilience. We explore strategies for pharmaceutical companies to adopt responsible sourcing practices, addressing environmental, social, and governance considerations in the procurement of raw materials and components.

The Era of Value-Based Healthcare

Transition to Value-Based Models

The transition to value-based healthcare models presents both challenges and opportunities. We discuss how pharmaceutical companies can align with value-based initiatives, emphasizing the demonstration of product value, outcomes-based pricing, and collaboration with healthcare payers.

Health Economic Outcomes Research (HEOR)

Health Economic Outcomes Research (HEOR) is integral to value-based healthcare. We explore the role of HEOR in pharmaceutical decision-making, including the generation of real-world evidence, economic modeling, and health technology assessments that inform market access and reimbursement strategies.

Crisis Preparedness and Management

Proactive Crisis Preparedness

The pharmaceutical industry must be prepared to navigate crises effectively. We discuss proactive crisis preparedness, encompassing risk assessments, scenario planning, and the development of robust crisis management strategies that safeguard corporate reputation and stakeholder trust.

Stakeholder Communication in Times of Crisis

Effective communication is central to crisis management. We provide guidance on transparent and empathetic stakeholder communication during crises, emphasizing the importance of maintaining trust, providing accurate information, and demonstrating a commitment to resolution.

The Future Landscape: Seizing Opportunities

As we conclude this guide, we encourage pharmaceutical professionals to view challenges as opportunities for growth and innovation. By proactively addressing regulatory complexities, promoting healthcare access, embracing technological disruptions, adapting to patient empowerment, ensuring supply chain resilience, navigating value-based healthcare, and mastering crisis management, stakeholders can contribute to shaping a resilient and impactful future for the pharmaceutical industry.

Embark on a journey of navigating challenges and seizing opportunities in the ever-evolving pharmaceutical landscape. As the industry pioneers, transformative initiatives and adapts to emerging trends, professionals play a vital role in advancing healthcare, driving innovation, and contributing to the well-being of global communities.

CHAPTER 13: ETHICAL DIMENSIONS IN PHARMACEUTICAL MARKETING

Upholding Integrity in an Evolving Landscape

As pharmaceutical marketing evolves, maintaining ethical standards is paramount to fostering trust among stakeholders and ensuring the industry's long-term sustainability. Chapter fourteen delves into the ethical dimensions of pharmaceutical marketing, exploring the principles, challenges, and strategies for upholding integrity.

Foundations of Ethical Marketing

The chapter begins by establishing the foundational principles that underpin ethical pharmaceutical marketing. It explores the importance of transparency, truthfulness, and patient-centricity as core elements that guide ethical decision-making. Real-world examples showcase instances where adherence to ethical principles positively impacted a company's reputation and relationships.

Navigating Regulatory Compliance

Ethical marketing goes hand in hand with regulatory compliance. This section examines the complex landscape of pharmaceutical regulations, emphasizing the need for marketers to stay abreast of local and international guidelines. Case studies highlight instances where companies successfully navigated regulatory challenges while maintaining ethical standards.

Responsible Data Usage and Privacy

In an era of data-driven marketing, the ethical use of data is a critical consideration. The chapter explores best practices for responsible data collection, storage, and usage, ensuring that patient privacy remains a top priority. It also addresses emerging concerns related to data breaches and the importance of building robust cybersecurity measures.

Balancing Profitability and Patient Welfare

Ethical pharmaceutical marketing requires striking a delicate balance between business objectives and patient welfare. This section discusses the challenges associated with profit-driven motives and explores strategies for aligning commercial success with societal well-being. Case studies illustrate instances where companies prioritized patient outcomes without compromising financial viability.

Ethics in Digital Marketing and Social Media

As digital channels play an increasingly significant role in pharmaceutical marketing, ethical considerations in the digital space are imperative. The chapter explores the ethical use of social media, online content, and influencer collaborations. It also addresses challenges such as misinformation and strategies for fostering transparent and responsible digital engagement.

Corporate Social Responsibility (CSR) in Marketing

Pharmaceutical companies are increasingly embracing corporate social responsibility as a core tenet of their operations. This section delves into the ethical dimensions of CSR initiatives, from community engagement to environmental sustainability. Case studies showcase successful CSR campaigns that not only benefited communities but also enhanced brand reputation.

Ethical Challenges in Global Marketing

In an era of globalized markets, navigating ethical challenges across diverse cultural contexts is essential. The chapter explores cultural nuances, ethical dilemmas in international marketing, and strategies for maintaining a universal commitment to ethical practices while respecting cultural diversity.

Building an Ethical Organizational Culture

The chapter concludes by emphasizing the role of organizational culture in fostering ethical behavior. It provides insights into cultivating a culture where ethical decision-making is ingrained at every level. Practical tips and case studies demonstrate how companies can create an environment that encourages employees to prioritize ethical considerations in their day-to-day activities.

Sustaining Trust for Future Success

Chapter fourteen serves as a compass for pharmaceutical marketers, guiding them through the ethical complexities of the industry. By prioritizing integrity, embracing regulatory compliance, and adopting responsible marketing practices, organizations can not only sustain trust but also contribute to the positive perception of the pharmaceutical industry as a whole.

CHAPTER 14: FUTURE HORIZONS IN PHARMACEUTICAL MARKETING

Anticipating and Shaping the Road Ahead

As pharmaceutical marketing continues its dynamic evolution, chapter fifteen explores the future horizons that will shape the industry in the coming years. From emerging technologies to evolving consumer behaviors, this chapter serves as a strategic guide for pharmaceutical marketers to anticipate and navigate the road ahead.

The Era of Precision Medicine

Precision medicine is poised to revolutionize healthcare and, by extension, pharmaceutical marketing. This section delves into the implications of personalized treatment approaches on marketing strategies. It explores how pharmaceutical companies can tailor their messaging and engagement to align with the individualized nature of precision medicine, creating targeted and impactful campaigns.

Artificial Intelligence and Predictive Analytics

The integration of artificial intelligence (AI) and predictive analytics is transforming the way pharmaceutical marketers operate. The chapter examines how AI can enhance data-driven decision-making, optimize targeting strategies, and streamline customer engagement. Real-world examples showcase the successful implementation of AI in predicting market trends and adapting marketing approaches accordingly.

Virtual and Augmented Reality Experiences

Immersive technologies like virtual reality (VR) and augmented reality (AR) are becoming integral tools in pharmaceutical marketing. This section explores how VR and AR can be leveraged to enhance medical education, patient engagement, and product visualization. Case studies illustrate innovative campaigns that successfully utilized these technologies to create memorable and impactful brand experiences.

Rise of Patient Empowerment

Empowered patients are becoming active participants in their healthcare journey. This chapter analyzes the shift toward patient-centricity and the role of informed and engaged patients in shaping pharmaceutical marketing strategies. It explores how companies can foster meaningful patient relationships through education, support programs, and digital platforms that empower individuals to make informed decisions about their health.

Blockchain in Healthcare and Marketing

Blockchain technology holds transformative potential in ensuring transparency, traceability, and security in healthcare data. The discussion delves into the applications of blockchain in pharmaceutical marketing, from supply chain integrity to patient data protection. Case studies showcase early adopters who have successfully integrated blockchain to enhance trust and accountability in their marketing practices.

Environmental Sustainability and Corporate Citizenship

As societal expectations evolve, environmental sustainability and corporate citizenship are becoming central to brand reputation. This section explores how pharmaceutical companies can align their marketing strategies with sustainable practices, emphasizing ethical sourcing, reduced environmental impact, and corporate social responsibility. Case studies highlight successful campaigns that resonate with environmentally conscious consumers.

Innovations in Multichannel Marketing

Multichannel marketing continues to evolve, integrating traditional and digital channels for a seamless customer experience. The chapter explores emerging trends in multichannel marketing, including the integration of Chabot's, voice-activated technologies, and cross-platform analytics. It provides insights into how pharmaceutical marketers can stay ahead by optimizing their presence across diverse channels.

Global Collaboration for Public Health

The future of pharmaceutical marketing involves increased

collaboration on a global scale. This section examines the potential for cross-border partnerships, knowledge exchange, and joint initiatives to address global health challenges. It explores how companies can engage in collaborative efforts that not only benefit public health but also contribute to positive brand perception on a global stage.

Charting a Course for Tomorrow

Chapter fifteen serves as a compass for pharmaceutical marketers navigating the evolving landscape of the industry. By anticipating and embracing emerging trends, technologies, and societal shifts, organizations can not only stay ahead but actively shape the future of pharmaceutical marketing, contributing to improved healthcare outcomes and positive patient experiences.

CONCLUSION

In concluding this comprehensive guide, "The Pharma Marketing Blueprint: Crafting Compelling Campaigns," we reflect on the dynamic and evolving landscape of pharmaceutical marketing and the imperative for professionals to navigate the future with foresight and innovation.

Embracing a Transformative Paradigm

The pharmaceutical industry is undergoing a transformative paradigm shift, marked by rapid technological advancements, evolving patient expectations, and a heightened focus on value-based healthcare. In this concluding chapter, we underscore the key takeaways that can guide pharmaceutical marketers in shaping their strategies and staying ahead in this ever-changing environment.

Adaptability as a Cornerstone

Embracing adaptability is fundamental to success. As the industry witnesses' technological disruptions, regulatory changes, and shifts in patient dynamics, marketers must cultivate a culture of flexibility. The ability to pivot, innovate, and swiftly respond to emerging trends will define the success of pharmaceutical marketing campaigns.

Patient-Centricity as a Guiding Principle

The empowered and informed patient is at the center of the new healthcare ecosystem. Our exploration of patient-centric approaches emphasizes the importance of building campaigns that resonate with the values, needs, and preferences of the modern healthcare consumer. By placing patients at the forefront, marketers can foster meaningful connections and drive positive health outcomes.

Technological Integration for Impact

Technological integration is not just a choice but a necessity. The chapters dedicated to digital transformation and cybersecurity underscore the pivotal role of technology in pharmaceutical marketing. From leveraging data analytics for targeted campaigns to safeguarding sensitive information, technology is a powerful ally that can amplify the effectiveness and reach of marketing initiatives.

Navigating Regulatory Complexities

The pharmaceutical landscape is intricately tied to regulatory frameworks. In our exploration of regulatory complexities, we highlight the need for marketers to stay informed, engage proactively with regulatory bodies, and build campaigns that align with evolving standards. Navigating regulatory challenges is integral to ensuring compliance and maintaining the integrity of marketing strategies.

Building Resilient Supply Chains

The disruptions experienced in global supply chains underscore the importance of resilience. Our discussion on supply chain challenges and sustainable practices emphasizes the role of marketers in advocating for responsible sourcing and fostering supply chain resilience. A robust and ethical supply chain contributes not only to business continuity but also to the industry's broader sustainability goals.

Value-Based Healthcare as a Driver

The transition to value-based healthcare models presents both challenges and opportunities. In our examination of value-based initiatives, we encourage marketers to align their strategies with the principles of demonstrating product value, engaging in outcomes-based pricing, and collaborating with stakeholders across the healthcare continuum.

Crisis Preparedness for Reputation Management

Proactive crisis preparedness is a non-negotiable aspect of pharmaceutical marketing. As explored in the chapters on crisis management, effective communication, and stakeholder trust, marketers play a crucial role in safeguarding the reputation of their organizations. Transparent and empathetic communication during times of crisis builds resilience and fosters long-term stakeholder loyalty.

A Call to Action

As we conclude this blueprint for pharmaceutical marketing, we issue a resounding call to action. The future of the industry is shaped by the collective efforts of visionary professionals who embrace change, prioritize ethical practices, and champion the well-being of patients and communities. The journey ahead is dynamic, and success lies in the hands of those who dare to innovate, lead with purpose, and navigate the intricate terrain of pharmaceutical marketing with resilience and integrity.

This guide serves as a compass for marketers navigating the complexities of the pharmaceutical landscape. Armed with insights, strategies, and a commitment to excellence, pharmaceutical professionals can craft compelling campaigns that not only drive business success but contribute to a healthier and more equitable future for all.

Embark on the journey of transformative pharmaceutical marketing, where each campaign becomes a beacon of positive change in the realm of healthcare. The future awaits, and with it, endless possibilities for those ready to shape the narrative of pharmaceutical marketing in the years to come.

Case Study 1: Leveraging Digital Health Platforms for Patient Engagement

Challenge: A pharmaceutical company aimed to enhance patient engagement and adherence for a chronic disease medication.

Solution: The company developed a mobile health app providing personalized medication reminders, educational resources, and a communication platform for patients and healthcare providers. The app utilized data analytics to tailor content to individual patient needs. The campaign resulted in a significant increase in medication adherence, improved patient satisfaction, and valuable real-world data for future drug development.

Case Study 2: Value-Based Pricing in Oncology Therapeutics

Challenge: A pharmaceutical company sought to navigate the transition to value-based healthcare and address market access challenges for its new oncology drug.

Solution: The company implemented a value-based pricing model, tying drug reimbursement to patient outcomes. Collaborating with payers, the company demonstrated the drug's effectiveness in improving patient survival rates. The initiative led to successful market access negotiations, aligning the drug's cost with its demonstrated value, and securing a competitive position in the market.

Case Study 3: Crisis Management in a Product Recall

Challenge: A pharmaceutical company faced a product recall due to potential safety concerns, risking damage to its reputation and stakeholder trust.

Solution: The company implemented a comprehensive crisis management plan, including transparent communication with regulatory bodies, healthcare providers, and patients. They provided clear information on the recall, reasons behind it, and steps taken to address the issue. Timely and transparent communication helped rebuild trust, and the company implemented enhanced quality control measures to prevent future recalls.

Case Study 4: Sustainable Supply Chain Practices

Challenge: A pharmaceutical company aimed to strengthen its supply chain resilience and adopt sustainable and ethical sourcing practices.

Solution: The company implemented a supply chain sustainability initiative, assessing and auditing suppliers for ethical practices, environmental impact, and social responsibility. They collaborated with suppliers to improve sustainability metrics and reduce the environmental footprint. The initiative not only enhanced supply chain resilience but also positioned the company as a leader in responsible sourcing.

Case Study 5: Patient Advocacy Partnership for Rare Disease Treatment

Challenge: A pharmaceutical company developed a breakthrough treatment for a rare disease but faced challenges in patient access due to the high cost of the medication.

Solution: The company collaborated with patient advocacy groups to create a patient assistance program, providing financial support, and worked with insurers to establish tiered pricing models. The partnership empowered patients to access the treatment, improved public perception, and demonstrated the company's commitment to addressing unmet medical needs.

These case studies highlight diverse challenges faced by pharmaceutical companies and the innovative solutions they employed to address them. Each case underscores the importance of strategic thinking, stakeholder collaboration, and a commitment to ethical and patient-centric practices in the dynamic landscape of the pharmaceutical industry.

ABOUT THE AUTHOR

Sales and Marketing Professional with more than 25 Plus years of diversified experience for both transnational and national pharmaceutical companies such as Merck & Co. Inc. NV Organon, AkzoNobel, and OBS Pakistan (Pvt.) Limited. Moreover, he is a university Professor and has more than 10 years' experience of teaching, research and supervising dissertations for MBA, MS. M.Phil., and Ph.D. level students. He is an author and coauthor of more than 200 publications, in which he has written more than 80 impact factor research articles, and 20 books.

www.ingramcontent.com/pod-product-compliance
Lightning Source LLC
Chambersburg PA
CBHW071059290526
45795CB00004B/1578